I Will Speak Your Name

Written & Illustrated

By

Danice E. Sweet

Pearson Publishing Company
Corpus Christi
2009

Copyright © 2009 by Danice E. Sweet

All rights reserved. No part of this book may be reproduced or transmitted in any form or by any means, electronic or mechanical, including photocopy, recording, or any information and storage and retrieval system, without prior written permission from the publisher, except by a reviewer who may quote brief passages in a review.

Library of Congress Control Number: 2009924045

ISBN-13: 978-0-9818480-4-4 perfect bound

ISBN-13: 978-0-9818480-5-1 e-book

Also available as a Kindle book on Amazon.com.

Cover Art: Danice E. Sweet
Cover design: Katherine Pearson Jagoe Massey
Book design: Katherine Pearson Jagoe Massey
Cover production: Tamara Teas, Information Data Systems

Published by
Pearson Publishing Company
Corpus Christi, Texas
www.PearsonPub.US

Dedication

This book is lovingly dedicated to my father, Jacob Clover. No man has ever worked harder, sweated more, and raised his daughters, his grandchildren, and his great-grandchildren, with more hope, and longing that they follow after God.

Thank you, Dad, for loving and caring for Mom, and for us. We are blessed to see Jesus in you.

Danice Sweet

Special Thanks

      To my friend, Laura Ehler, for her wisdom, humor, and for proofreading, and being a wonderful sounding board when I needed one.

      To those who have supported our gospel music group, Revival: I can't believe we've been blessed to have the opportunity to praise the Lord together for twenty years.

Table of Contents

Foreword		xiii
Suggestions for Using This Book		xv
Chapter One	I Still Do	1
Chapter Two	More Fun Than Cardboard	5
Chapter Three	Life Is Like A Rollercoaster	9
Chapter Four	Who Left That in the Sink?	13
Chapter Five	You Done Flung Your Cravin' On Me	17
Chapter Six	Happy Alloween	21
Chapter Seven	The Cat Who Hissed At Winter	25
Chapter Eight	T-Boned	29
Chapter Nine	A City on A Hill	33
Chapter Ten	He's Lord of All	37
Chapter Eleven	I'm No Picasso	41
Chapter Twelve	I'm Giving You Pearls	45
Chapter Thirteen	It Ain't Over	49
Chapter Fourteen	Do You Believe?	53
Chapter Fifteen	Slip Sliding Away	57
Chapter Sixteen	Thank God for Kids	61
Chapter Seventeen	Time For Some Pruning	65
Chapter Eighteen	Sing It Out	69
Chapter Nineteen	Cat Herding	73
Chapter Twenty	Things to Do	77
Chapter Twenty-One	God's Grace and Gummy Worms	81
Afterword		85
Bibliography		89

Foreword

I've lost several dear friends to cancer. One precious sister in Christ, who I confided in during a time of frustration and turmoil, shared some words that have stuck with me.

"Never let anyone tell you where and when you can share the gospel. Christ has already done that."

Libby Sears was a woman who was graceful, dignified, and who loved the Lord. She shared those words with me while we were struggling to share the Good News in song. Her words, her faith, and her strength during her struggle with cancer have given me hope during some dark hours.

Barbara Carver, was a precious sister in Christ. I was so overwhelmed that I could not physically speak when I went to see her the last time in the hospital. I wept openly and asked God for the right words but couldn't utter a sound except for crying. She looked at me and smiled and said, "You don't have to say a thing. I just wanted to see you before I left. Don't cry for me. I'm going Home."

My uncle, Olen Ashlock, was a man after God's own heart. He had a smile as big as Texas, a shoulder to cry on, and words of wisdom to hold on to.

My uncle, Carl Hardy, had a quick wit and a word of encouragement. Knowing he was in my corner made this world a brighter place.

Our family lost them both this last year. They have given me two more reasons to look forward to Heaven.

Suggestions for Using This Book

As a personal devotional

In a Bible study setting

    Read the chapter
    Listen to the song on the CD
    Consider the questions for further reflection
    Pray

Chapter One
I Still Do

The value of an object varies due to its sentimentality, beauty, usefulness and its worth. I spent three hours yesterday searching for my wedding ring, ten year anniversary ring and gold watch. All were gifts from my husband, and on his fiftieth birthday, we were so busy cleaning the house for his party, that I misplaced them. I didn't worry about finding them, I knew they would eventually turn up. As an artist and musician, clutter and disorganization do not disturb me. In fact, I thrive on them. Not to the extent that I don't pick things up off the floor, well, okay, my husband did find one of my shoes under a night shirt today, but I can work and create in an environment that might cause others stress.

We had a great gathering of friends and several brought their guitars. We sang and played until our fingers and voices were tired. From John Denver favorites to Farther Along gospel standards, we jammed.

While cleaning up after the party, I remembered I had not located my rings and watch, so I said a prayer and began retracing my steps. Laundry room, guest bedroom, guitar and banjo cases, make-up bag. Nothing.

We headed to church Sunday morning, and it felt strange not to have my wedding ring or watch on. I determined that when I got home, I would really go on a jewelry hunt. My hunt turned into a Sunday afternoon nap and by evening, I was concerned.

Something kept telling me I should check the trash cans, so I went through every can in the house. This was not pleasant and actually quite gross. Although I love guacamole, I will not be able to enjoy avocados for a while.

My husband, Chet was determined to go through every counter, cabinet and cubby hole that I keep things in, and his persistence was not only unappreciated, it was annoying. You see, that's his gift. Not annoyance, but persistence. He's a perfectionist. He creates amazing woodwork with dovetail ends and precise Shaker style tables that thin as their legs reach the floor. When he runs the sound system for our Christian music group, Revival, every knob, every button is in place, and it makes all the difference.

While I retired to my nightly ritual of writing in my journal and poured out my anguish at the loss of my most treasured keepsakes, he began rifling through the trash bags outside in the dark of night. I was beginning to feel like the woman, in the parable that Jesus told, who had lost a coin, like in *Luke 15: 8-10*.

He came in wreaking of garbage and knelt down beside the bed where I was crying and whispered, "Do you still love me?" "Of course, I do," I replied.

Then he laid my wedding ring of twenty-one years, and my anniversary ring of eleven years, and my watch in my hand. He found them, and cleaned them, and brought them to me. I was overwhelmed. I said, "I don't know how to tell you how much I appreciate this." He replied, "This was the best birthday gift I could have gotten."

Love isn't perfect. Marriage isn't perfect. Friendships aren't perfect. Relationships are painful. Families are flawed, and churches are made of humans who make mistakes. They have moments of anguish, heartache, and desperation. There are also hilltops, valleys, joys, and kindnesses that are never forgotten. Especially from that person you call when the biopsy hasn't come back yet; that cousin that mentored you through those horrible teen years, and still believes in you, (thank you, Tammy); that friend who has loved you through mistakes, miseries, and misguidedness.

For further reflection:

1. What unrealistic expectations do you have of yourself or someone in your life right now?

> *But store up for yourselves treasures in heaven, where moth and rust do not destroy, and where thieves do not break in and steal. For where your treasure is, there your heart will be also. Matthew 6:21. New International Version of the Bible (NIV).*

2. What promises do you find in Matthew 6:21?

3. Has someone done something for you that you did not expect?

Give Me Jesus

In the morning when I rise
In the morning when I rise, in the morning when I rise
Give me Jesus
Give me Jesus, give me Jesus
You can have all this world
Give me Jesus
And when I am alone
Oh, when I am alone, when I am alone
Give me Jesus
And when I come to die
When I come to die, When I come to die
Give me Jesus
Give me Jesus, Give me Jesus
Give me Jesus
Give me Jesus
You can have all this world,
Give me Jesus.

Prayer for the Day:

Father God,
Thank You for who You are and what You mean to my life.
Help me to see the good in those who are around me each day
and to let them know how much they mean to me.
In honor of Your son, Jesus of Nazareth.
Amen.

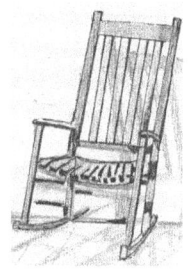

Chapter Two
More Fun Than Cardboard

    A friend called this evening and asked if I could come over for one of her famous cafe iced lattes. I normally don't like to drink something with caffeine in the evening, but I made an exception. As we were visiting, I was introduced to her brand new kitten, a seven week-old long-haired calico.

    If you haven't watched a playful kitten in a while, you are missing out. Somersaults, flips, tail-chasing, playing with any and everything that moved or hid in the shadows.

    I got so tickled seeing this little bright-eyed fur ball jump, play, and surprise herself. Everything from a pillow on the couch, to an air-conditioning vent on the floor was new undiscovered treasure.

    She finally succumbed to an afternoon of non-stop excitement and fell asleep with her little eyes giving me one last wink, good-bye. I left with a smile on my face and a reminder of a simple pleasure. I became like a little kid again with that little kitten.

    Reminds me of the words of Jesus when he said,

> *I tell you the truth, unless you change and become like little children, you will never enter the kingdom of Heaven.*
> *Matthew 18:2. NIV.*

    Little children look at each other and size each other up pretty quickly. They see someone their size, and assume that they can play together. We were at a workshop in Oklahoma, and my great nephew saw a boy his same height and immediately asked, "You want to play?"

They became fast friends, laughing, running and singing together. I have to say, there aren't many adults that can do that so instantly.

We bought my great nephews a "Kangaroo Climber" for Easter. It's a plastic piece of outdoor play equipment and has a slide and is a little four by four foot play house with a half door that our littlest one can pop his head through and say "Hi!" It took me an hour trying to put it together, and I gave up and asked my husband for help. It took him five minutes.

Mom and I were so proud of the gift and couldn't wait to see their response when they looked in our backyard to see the new play equipment. The fun lasted about thirty minutes, then the spring wind drove us all inside.

Sitting in the corner of the sunroom was the cardboard box the "Climber" came in. We played with it for at least two hours. My husband got in the box, the boys got in the box, we closed the box, covered the box, opened the box, pounded on the box. Who knew a box could be so much fun? I should have bought a cardboard box.

That's the way it works sometimes. You put so much time and thought into a gift or idea and you forgot the most important thing. Just being together.

I was asked to write a song for a special occasion. I stared down at my hands and feet and thought about the gifts God has given and was so filled with gratitude. I was reminded of why we are here.

He Has Made Me

He has made me with two strong hands
He has made me with two good feet
How I use gifts He gave brings glory or brings shame
All I want to do is praise His name.

Even the stars shine the birds they sing their song
All of creation testifies
And since He calls me child He wants the world to know
We've got more than just our Father's eyes.

He has saved you with blood so dear
He has saved you the word made clear
How you use the gifts He gave brings glory or brings shame
He just wants to hear you praise His name:
Emmanuel, God is with us.

For further reflection:

1. Do you recall a time when an event was planned down to the minute, and it didn't work out as planned?

2. How can you include God in your daily plans?

> *Since, then, you have been raised with Christ, set your hearts on things above, where Christ is seated at the right hand of God. Colossians 3:1. NIV.*

3. What is one way that you set your mind on things above?

Prayer for the Day:

Dear Heavenly Father,
I just want to stop what I'm doing right now and thank You.
For the stars, the sun, the moon, the rain and even the Kansas wind.
Thank You for putting me here for a reason.
In the holy name of our wonderful Savior, Emmanuel.
Amen.

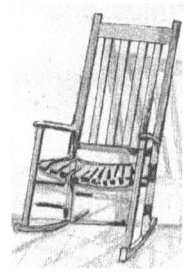

Chapter Three
Life Is Like A Rollercoaster

> *Thy word is a lamp unto my feet and a light unto my path.*
> *Psalm 119:105. NIV.*

I've read that passage many times and sung the song with gusto. It just seemed so clear to me, when I read it last night, like understanding it for the first time.

When we can't see clearly, it's because we're not in His word. If we stumble on the path, we've got to get closer to the light. Just like walking at night without a flashlight, we can't see what we're on, in, or coming up to.

I was riding a rollercoaster as a teenager with my father at the Worlds of Fun in Kansas City. It was the first week of the season for the park, and we felt lots of excitement as we were standing in line for the rollercoaster that was the fastest in the country at the time.

We got on the seats, and they locked us in, and we started up the first incline. I was looking over at my dad as it picked up speed, when suddenly the centrifugal force caused my head to start bouncing back and forth in between the padded bar that keeps you in place. I tried with all my strength to push my head back where it was supposed to be, but the momentum kept me from doing it.

Just as we ascended another hill, an overgrown branch from a tall tree, whacked me right up side the head. Everyone was screaming and laughing while I was just screaming. I had expected the ride of a lifetime but not the end of my life. I haven't been on a rollercoaster since that day.

We don't always get what we expect. The picture sometimes looks better than the real thing. Life is like a rollercoaster: there are ups and downs and sometimes you scream. Occasionally you're breathless, and often you're scared of what is around the corner. Sometimes you just wish it would end. Once in a while you hope for a second time around.

We heard a children's group sing in Conroe, Texas years ago. I was so impressed with their harmony, I was determined to get them in a recording studio and get their beautiful voices on tape. That group called themselves, Revelation. We recorded an album with them called, *Under Construction*. I began writing songs so they would have some original music for the album. This was one of those songs.

God Made Everything

He made the monkey and the coconut
He made the palm tree, too
He made the ocean and the octopus and
He made me and you

He makes me laugh and He makes me sing
He gives me everything I need
He even made the air I breathe
My God made everything

He made the moose and the mountain goat
He made the rivers, too
He made the forests and the antelope
And He made me and you

He made the leopard and the elephant
He made the cockatoo
He made the monkey and orangutan
And He made me and you

The armadillo and the prairie dog
He made the cactus, too
He made the rabbit and the porcupine
And He made the skunk too, pew

He makes me laugh and he makes me sing
He gives me everything I need
He even made the air I breathe
My God made everything

For further reflection:

> *For it is God who is at work within you....*
> *Philippians 2:12. NIV.*

1. In what way do you need to accept how he has made you?

2. In what way can you change areas of your life, your body or relationships so that you become more like Him?

Prayer for the Day:

El Shaddai,
You are above all and in all
You are mighty beyond the powers of this Earth.
You have a plan, and had a plan before time began.
I trust in you.
I trust in your wisdom.
Though I don't understand your sacrifice, I'm grateful for it.
In the wonderful name of Jesus,
Amen.

Chapter Four
Who Left That in the Sink?

I have a friend I work with who is a bright spot in the day. Her smile lights up an entire school building. Whenever I see her, which is usually, once a week, I want to be around her. I want to be more like her. I want to shine like a light on hill.

Too often I'm not even a nightlight, I'm not even a flicker, perhaps that spark that flint makes when you hit it with metal a few times. I was a Campfire girl. No, I didn't make campfires or have a fascination with fire, well okay a little one. It was like Girl Scouts, but different. We didn't go on any trips, or sell cookies. We just sold overpriced candy and made really awful crafts. We put stick pins in Styrofoam balls to attach glass beads for a Christmas ornament. I wouldn't trust kids with stick pins today, or glass beads. Styrofoam balls , maybe.

The other day, I had two ceramic coffee mugs in my art class that students kept using to put water in for watercolors. I had asked them to use the recycled plastic Jell-O cups, but a few didn't hear.

I didn't want these mugs to break on our hard floor, so I took them to the teacher's workroom and put them in the sink. I ran some water in them to soak, and hopefully remove the watercolor stains, and had to run back to my classroom since students were on their way. I had the intention of going back after my next class and cleaning the cups out.

Lunch time arrived before I did, however, and someone wrote a note in red ink, asking "Do we not have time to clean up after ourselves?"

Feeling a little ornery, I decided to write, on the same note in red ink, "If you have time to write this note, then you had more time than I did to clean out these cups."

So the discussion among my coworkers was who wrote this note and who left the cups. I was quiet as long as I could be (30 seconds, those of you who know me) and then 'fessed up to leaving the cups, and explained my reasoning for writing the note. There was a chuckle and that was that. Guess I could have quoted I Corinthians 3:8:

> *It's not the one who plants or the one who waters who is at the center of this process, but God, who makes things grow.*
> *I Corinthians 3:8. MSG.*

The next day at lunch. My friend...the light on the hill, said, "I don't know what happened yesterday, but someone was very upset by the simple request I made, asking that we clean up after ourselves." All the eyes in the room looked at her, then at me, and I had to confess once again, that I had written the reply hastily, on a bad day. We all laughed and realized it was a series of errors.

However, I realized that I have disappointed my friend at my hasty response. The impression I hoped to leave at the workplace was not dirty cups in the sink. Nor was it the impression of someone who doesn't care. But the impression of a caring and concerned teacher doing her best.

For further reflection:

1. How is God using you in the workplace to show someone Jesus?

2. Think about a time when you have fallen. Have you forgiven yourself?

3. Have you ever done something that changed someone's impression of you?

Prayer for the Day:

Jehovah,
I'm not sure what Your will is.
I'm not sure why
I am in Your plans at all,
but I'm grateful I am.
Thank You for calling me Your child,
and letting me call You Father.
In the name of Your precious son, Jesus Christ.
Amen

Chapter Five
You Done Flung Your Cravin' On Me

I was chewing spearmint gum in our Suburban on a long road trip when I asked the friends in the backseat if they wanted a piece of gum. One replied, "You done flung your cravin' on me!"

I said, "What?"

He repeated himself, "You done flung your cravin' on me!"

Now, I've traveled from Augusta, Georgia, to Dauphin, Manitoba, Canada and from Kiev, Ukraine to London, England, and I've heard some strange sayings. But I had never heard that reply. I had to have it explained, twice, as I recall.

It's like when you smell microwave popcorn, and you want some, even if you weren't hungry at all before it started cooking. Then you decide it should be illegal to cook something that smells up an entire office or home and not share it with the people working in the same said office.

Has anyone ever flung their cravin' on you? You weren't even thinking of food, or a friend, or a problem or gossiping, and once that word or name is in the air, it just hangs there.

Why is it, that you can have the best intentions, and then once someone starts talking about someone in a negative way, those memories come back of how that person hurt you, and boom! Out it comes: a put down, a comment that can't be taken back, and you regret it ever coming out of your mouth.

> *God wants you to mature, God doesn't want his children holding grudges.*
> *Philippians 4:2. The Message Bible (MSG)*

> *With each of you we were like a father, with his child, holding your hand, whispering encouragement, showing you step by step, how to live well before God who called you into His own kingdom, into this delightful life.*
> *I Thessalonians 2:11. MSG.*

> *So come on, let's leave finger-painting exercises on Christ and get on with the grand work of art.*
> *Hebrews 6:1. MSG.*

I love the way The Message Bible phrases Hebrews 6:1.

As an artist, and art teacher of children, I've seen the look on a five year-old's face when they have their hands in paint. It's like a 'hand caught in the cookie jar' face times ten! You mean I get to put my hands in paint and put it on paper? This is okay? "ALL RIGHT!"

A first grader stated it this way, "This was my bestest day ever, I got to paint!" I'll never forget his grin. Total joy.

The Hebrew writer says, there's a place for that, but now we must move on to creating a masterpiece. Masterpieces take time. It took Michelangelo over four years to paint the Sistine Chapel, on his back. The main panels down the center depict scenes from the Book of Genesis, from the Creation, to the Fall of Adam and Eve, and to Noah's deluge, with over three hundred figures in the painting.

Sometimes I wish God could change a situation or circumstance immediately. I forget that things take time. God is at work before we even know to ask for His help. I want the picture in my life to change like a digital camera. Point, shoot, erase, start over.

My students ask hundreds of times a day, "Do you like my picture?" Sometimes I ask them in return, "How do *you* like it? Did you do your best?" "If you had more time would you add anything extra?" Then I realize, all they really want is approval. They want to know they've "done good."

Whether it is for a meal that was met with an enthusiastic response, a painting that someone connects with and wants in their home, or a child that says, "Love you Shun-shine," that can warm your heart for weeks. We all seek approval, be it a pat on the back, or applause, we want to be wanted.

For further reflection:

1. What truth in God's word have you seen or heard or read today? Whatever you do, work at it with all your heart as working for the Lord, not for men.

2. Read Colossians 3:15. How does it relate to your life today?

> *Let the peace of Christ rule in your hearts, since as members of one body you were called to peace. And be thankful.*
> *Colossians 3:15. NIV.*

3. What is one habit you want to break, so you'll be a better friend?

After going through a heart breaking struggle, I received a beautiful quote from a friend. It said, "Sometimes God calms the storms, sometimes God calms His child and lets the storm rage on." This gave me peace. I realized the storm was going to keep raging, but God could give me peace in the middle of it. That inspired this song.

I Will Speak Your Name

I will speak Your name when the storm is raging
I will speak Your name when the sea is calm
I will speak Your name when my fears o'ertake me
And forever on my lips, I will speak Your name

You are my God, a help in time of trouble
And my source of my salvation
And forever in my heart You will remain
I will speak Your name

You are my King, and I'm here to serve You
And I sing praises to the Lamb

And the riches of this world I shall not claim
For I will speak Your name
Well why can't You answer
In words I understand
And I can't make sense of all Your plans
I will still speak Your name

Prayer for the Day:

Dear Lord,
You are mighty in all Your ways.
Your hand sustains me, protects me, and guides me.
Help me to react to others more like Your son Jesus did.
It's in His name I pray,
Amen.

Chapter Six
Happy Alloween

I just stopped off at our local grocery store to get a few things and when I walked out the door, I saw that a car wash on the corner had a sign that said, "Happy Alloween."

I immediately acknowledged that the "H" must have fallen off Halloween in our Kansas wind, and then I looked up again.

"Happy Alloween."

Maybe there never was an H. Maybe the car wash attendant was a writer. Happy *All*oween: A holiday where anything goes, ghosts, skeletons, tombstones, a celebration of death, a season of scary, an autumn of awful.

I love fall, but I've never loved Halloween, though I've enjoyed more than my share of trick or treat bags with popcorn balls and snack size snickers. I don't like being scared. I don't like scary movies. Even as a kid, I remember going door to door in my costumes and thinking wouldn't this be easier if we just went to the store?

Country singer Martina McBride is a Kansas girl. She had a huge number one hit with the song, Independence Day. It starts out talking about a girl who turned eight years old one summer in the midst of a dysfunctional family. It caused me to reflect on my eighth birthday and the decision I made to be baptized. I was so young, but so determined that I could not wait another day. In a beautiful, college town in Emporia, Kansas on a Sunday evening, I stepped out into the aisle of the church and knew without a doubt it was time.

That action inspired this song I wrote.
Spiritual Life

I was eight years old that Sunday
When I heard the preacher say
The water's just right, come and change your life
Come forward and we'll show you the way
I didn't know where my feet were going
Wild horses couldn't keep me away
You know I made up my mind and the time was right
To be born again that day

Spiritual life He's given
And I'm takin' every step by faith
Spiritual life I'm livin' following Him closer each day
Well I've never been perfect
And I don't claim to be
But I've never ever had to think twice
Since I gave my soul to Jesus
I've been living this spiritual life.

I had turned eighteen that evening
When he gave me the key to his heart
But when push came to shove
There was no compromise
You know I said no right from the start
I had made a decision beforehand but it never was a sacrifice
But since I said yes to Jesus
You know I've been livin' this spiritual life

She was seventy-eight that evening
They said she's lucky if she's here through the night
Family and friends are all gathered around
In the distance she could see the bright light
Angels they were singin' they were callin' from the other side
She said she's ready to go to Heaven
Where she'll keep living this spiritual life
You know I'm a-living this spiritual life

For further reflection:

> *Since we live by the Spirit, let us keep in step with the Spirit.*
> *Galatians 5:25. NIV.*

1. What unrealistic expectation do you have of yourself or someone in your life right now?

2. In what areas do you know you need to grow?

Prayer for the Day:

Almighty Father,
You amaze me with Your power, Your love,
and the beauty that surrounds me each day.
Thank You for today.
Thank You for Your son, Jesus.
Amen.

Chapter Seven
The Cat Who Hissed at Winter

Our Kansas winter began in fall this year. The temperature went from eighty degrees to thirty degrees in one day. Our calico cat, Callie, cried and cried at the front door, begging to go outside. When we opened the door, she stepped outside, hissed and ran back into the warmth of our home. I couldn't help but giggle. Her reaction was similar to mine at times. I don't vocalize a hiss, but a sigh and sometimes even a moan.

When the cold wind blows, and trials come, and my joints ache, my spirit wonders how long this journey on Earth will take. When my great nephew, Noah, picks up an aerosol can, he goes "HISSS." He knows what the can sounds like, but also knows he's not supposed to push it.

My knees popped as I got up from the couch last week, and my great nephew, Gabriel, said, "Ne-Ne, was that you?" "Yes," I replied. "Did that hurt?" he asked. "A little bit," I answered. When the dishes need done, the laundry piles up, or the bills are the only thing in the mailbox, I groan.

It's hard to face each day with it's list of chores, papers, work, classes, and cleaning and know that you'll do the same thing tomorrow. So how do you wake up with the same "umph" to make it through the day?

I'm reminded of the scripture in Galatians that says, "Do not grow weary in well doing." Easier said than done. Especially when you feel like you are the only one doing the "well doing." Does anyone else ever change the toilet paper roll? My husband says "yes." I have to admit he is the first to apologize, the first to clean up even if I left something, and the first to take care of something that needs done without being asked.

You have no idea hard that was for me to write. But it's true. He is a counselor and caregiver and has a soft side that few people get to see. He truly cares about how people feel and how they respond to things that are said. I wish I was more like him in that area.

For further reflection:

1. Are you dealing with divorce, health issues, addiction, or poor finances?

2. What is conflicting with your desire to serve God?

3. What does Romans 7:15-19 say about these things?

Nothing Like the Feeling of Harmony

Well there's nothing like the feeling of harmony
Singing with my brothers as they sing with me
Liftin' up our praises to the King of kings
No there's nothing like the feeling of harmony
We might not be in the building or going door to door
We might not have our Sunday suits and praise the Lord
We hope you like the music, but pray there's something more
Liftin' up our voices singing one accord

No there's nothing like the feeling of harmony
Singing with my brothers as they sing with me
Liftin' up our praises to the King of kings
You know there's nothing like the feeling of harmony
You might prefer tradition or a soulful hymn
You might not like percussion nor to say "Amen"
But if the Lord is liftin' won't you join on in
And help us sing the chorus once again

> *He says, 'I will declare your name to my brothers; in the presence of the congregation I will sing your praises.'*
> *Hebrews 2:12. NIV.*

> *Finally brothers live in harmony one with another.*
> *I Peter 3:8. NIV.*

Prayer for the Day:

Our Father, who resides in Heaven,
Your name be praised and lifted high.
May Your will be done here on Earth
In my life and in those I love.
Thank You for providing us food to eat.
Please forgive us for the sins we commit,
In the same way we forgive others.
Keep us from temptation, and keep us from doing wrong.
To You all power, glory and honor are due
Forever and always.
Amen.

Chapter Eight
T-Boned

Mom called me on her cell phone today. She sounded frantic, nervous and scared. She said, "Call 911, your dad's been in an accident and the ambulance hasn't arrived yet. Meet me five miles north of town." My first instinct was to pray. I called 911, and they said someone was already en route.

I told my husband what mom had said and we got in the car and started praying. Praying for Dad, praying for Mom, praying for the paramedics, and for peace to deal with whatever happened.

We arrived as they were putting a brace on Dad's neck and putting him in the ambulance. All I could see was blood running down his face, and I knew I had to stay calm for Mom. The sheriff, trying to direct traffic around the accident said, "You can't park here, ma'am, you've got to move on."

I saw Mom's van and hopped out of the car to comfort her. Chet moved our car out of the way, and then I saw Dad's truck. It was not good. The sheriff came over and apologized, he said, "I didn't know that Jake was your Dad. We don't know how he walked away from this one. We got here, and he was trying to help the guy who 'T-Boned' his truck. The guy was a security guard, just got off work, and never saw Jake. He pulled out onto a 70 mph highway."

They took Dad by ambulance to our local hospital and several church members had seen the accident and thought it might have been Dad. Within ten minutes the Emergency Waiting Room was filled with family, friends and church members, and we started praying. The nurse came out and said, "There's just too many of you, and you are being too loud, you've got to move to another area."

Twenty people moved as one, like a huddle at the fifty yard line of a football game, and we waited to hear if Dad would walk again. In and out of the emergency room, praying and trying to remember when was the last time I told him I loved him. Now I tell him every time we say goodbye, so I don't have to wonder.

He's still sore, and has gone through physical therapy and has one more story to tell. He's walking, but his three year old great grandson beat him in a foot race last week, and Dad's still limping.

My mother was the youngest of ten children who grew up during the Depression. She always said she never wanted to disappoint her father. Not because of the punishment, but because she didn't want to see the look of disappointment on his face. That's what inspired this song. It means so much to me after nearly losing my dad far too soon.

I've Got A Father

Always tried to be home early not late
Didn't want to see the look on Daddy's face
When I walked through the door
And he'd been waiting on me
You see I wasn't afraid of any punishment
Just couldn't stand the thought I'd disappointed Daddy
One more time
And put a tear in his eye
You see he's the kind of father always hoped for the best
He was there for me when everyone left
And I've got a father
Don't want to let him down
He's got a faith in me
Farther than I can see
His love for me abounds
He's got plans and dreams
Of what he wants me to be
And I don't want to disappoint Daddy
'Cause I know he loves me
One day I'm going to make it to that heavenly gate
Can't wait to see the look on God's face
When I kneel down before
My one and only Lord
He'll wrap His arms around me, I'll climb on His knee

Put my hand on His shoulder, breathe a sigh of relief
At home I'll be
Eternally
You see He's the kind of Father never let me down
He's prepared for me a home and a crown

A long time ago a boy left home
Spent all the money he would ever own
Came to himself ready to give up
Then he pictured home and his father's love
I've got a Father
We've got a Father
You've got a Father
Don't want to let Him down

For further reflection:
1. In what way do you view God like your father?

> *So he got up and went to his father. But while he was still a long way off, his father saw him and was filled with compassion for him; he ran to his son, threw his arms around him and kissed him. Luke 15:20. NIV.*

2. In what ways is God different than your Earthly father?

Prayer for the Day:

Holy One,
You made the leaves to change, the snow to fall, and the sun to rise.
Help me to see Your hand today in my life and be grateful You care for me more than the sparrows. Thank You for the seasons and Most of all for the Lord of all creation, Jesus Christ.
Amen.

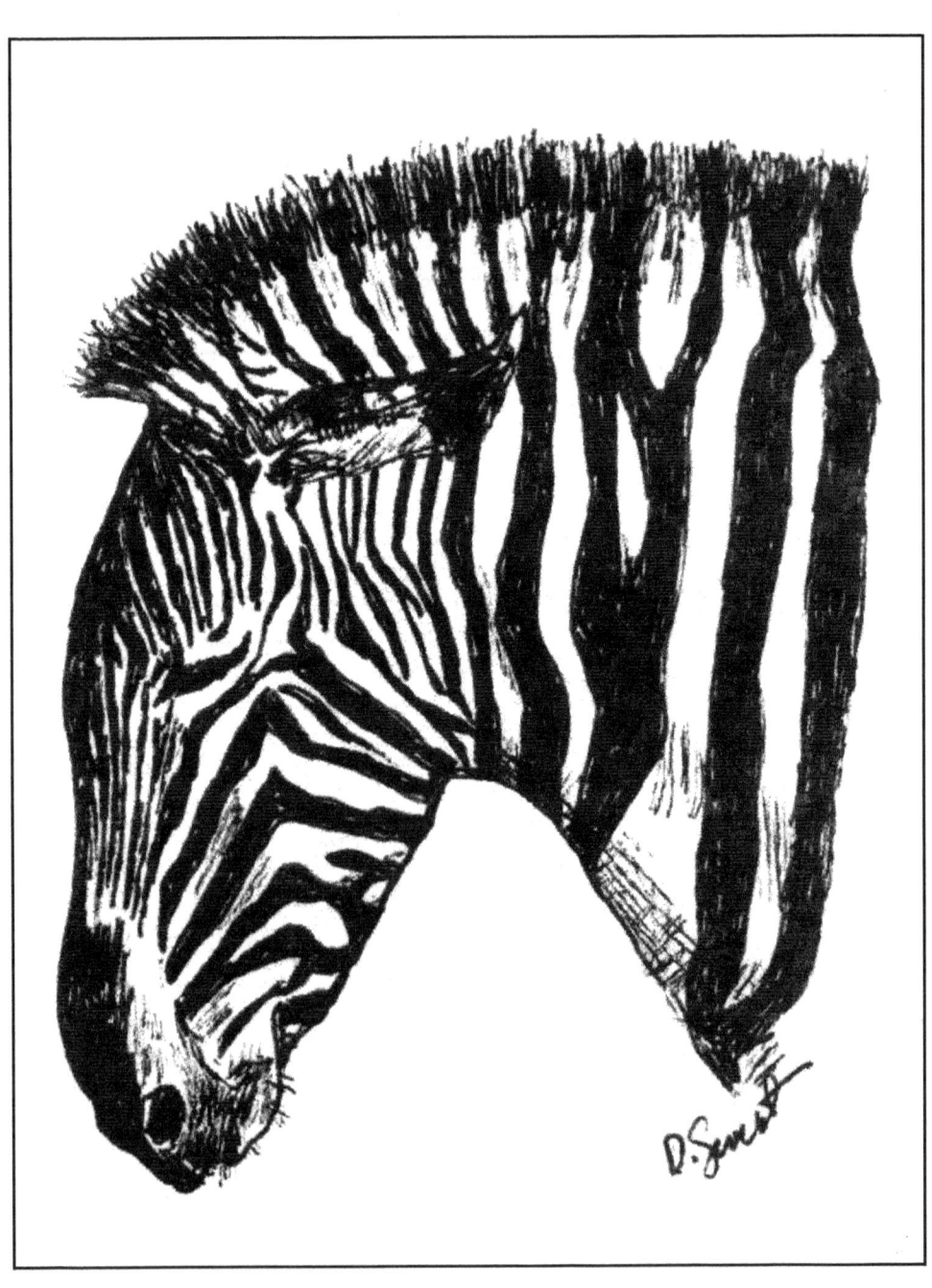

You know they say that a zebra's stripes are as unique as a thumbprint.
No two zebras are the same.

Chapter Nine
A City on a Hill

    I received two lamps Friday from a rummage sale my mom stopped by. They had Kelly green lamp shades, and our sun room is green, and my mom thought of me. I'm sure they looked right at home in some 1970's decor with huge rustic brown textured pottery like vases for bottoms. I probably wouldn't have picked them out of a store and taken them home. But your eyes change at a yard sale. Through all of the junk and unwanted clutter someone else is discarding, your eye spots a bargain, and you picture it in your own home.
    You see your vision changes at a yard sale. I don't know if it's the thought of getting a bargain, or beating someone to the deal of a lifetime, or if you picture yourself ending up on the Antiques Roadshow.
    Well, as soon as my husband got home, without a blink he said, "Those are some ugly lamps. You're not putting those in the sunroom we just redecorated are you?" Well actually yes, that was the plan, but I quickly replied, "No, of course not. I'm taking them to my art room at school, and we'll use them for creating shadows and highlights."
    Garage sales don't take returns, and I've got some bad lamps. Have you ever had a bad lamp? I've had several. One shocked me every time I turned it on. Another fell apart every time I pulled the chain.
    There's something within me that has trouble throwing things away. I'm not in the hoarder category like you see on Oprah, where people have a path through their house and have kept every newspaper since Kennedy was assassinated. But I do have trouble tossing

electronics, old cell phones, and bad lamps. I know I will never have them repaired, but I keep looking for someone who could use them. By now you may think I have a diagnosis.

> *When the light of the lamp shines on you...See to it then that the light within you is not darkness. Don't hide your light.*
> *Luke 11:35. NIV.*

What do you look for? The good, the light, the hope in others, or do you look for the negative, the dark? I know I've been a bad lamp at times. The light of Jesus was inside me but because of things I've said and done, it's so dim you couldn't light a room with it, much less my corner of the world.

I wonder who has been counting on my light to shine and has been stumbling in the darkness unable to see because I'm blocking out the light Christ said He put inside me.

> *A city on a hill cannot be hidden. Neither do people light a lamp and put it under a bowl. Instead they put it on its stand, and it gives light to everyone in the house.*
> *Matthew 5:14-15. NIV.*

Booker, a wonderful song leader and man of God I've looked up to for years, came to our home town many years ago to lead a singing workshop. He said this church is as it should be, on a hill so the whole city can see it's light. That has always stuck with me. If we are the church, how bright is our light shining for all to see?

When trouble comes, and the clouds are overcast, who do we depend on for light? Who do we run to? Where do we go first? On our knees, or to our e-mail or cell phone. I have to admit after the dust settles, and I've no where else to turn, I bow my head and start to pray.

I have a blue over-stuffed chair and ottoman that I paid fifty dollars for at a yard sale. Fifty dollars is a lot of money, especially for a yard sale. But this was a comfy looking blue pin striped chair. It was sitting in someone's driveway and called to me, "Come sit for a spell and try me out."

I hopped out of my car and sat down in the chair. Snug, comfortable, not too worn, it was perfect. I put my weary feet up and knew it would provide hours of comfort. I got the bargain of the day and was so proud of myself. I picked it up and shoved it into my vehicle and drove with the back window half way out so I could get it home.

I put it in our sun room, and I don't care if the sun fades it, or if my great nephews jump up and down on it, because it was a bargain. I've already got several summers out of it and feel proud even though it shows it's age. I've sat in it and watched the leaves turn from green to orange, and seen deer run through our backyard, as well as a gaggle of turkeys searching for refuge during hunting season.

Still no lamp in the room. I just come inside when it starts getting dark or let the lightning bugs light up the backyard.

For further reflection:

1. Has there been anyone in your life, a teacher or preacher or friend who has been a light at the end of your tunnel?

2. In what way have you shown your light to others?

My Lord Arose

My Lord arose
My Jesus walked on water and He walked on solid ground
He healed the lame, He made them walk, He's working even now
He sent the Holy Spirit and He comforts me each day
He intercedes for me each time I pray

My Lord arose
Up from the grave to conquer death
My Lord arose
Up on the third day filled with breath
He died, He rose , I'm going to meet Him and Heaven knows
The tomb is empty 'cause my Lord arose
My Jesus knows when I am happy, knows when I am sad
He knows when I am burdened and each trouble that I've had
He knows when I'm discouraged, even when I'm feeling low
Don't have to tell Him 'cause my Jesus knows

He gave up everything on Earth to save me from my sin
He said He's coming back so He can take me home with Him
I never have to doubt a single thing my Savior said
He rose again and is no longer dead

He arose a victor from the dark domain
And He lives forever with His saints to reign
He arose , He arose
Hallelujah Christ arose
The tomb is empty 'cause my Lord arose

> *Where, O death, is your victory? Where, O death, is your sting?*
> *I Corinthians 15:55. NIV.*

Prayer for the Day:

God over all the universe,
There are parts of my life that I need Your help with.
You know what they are, and so do I.
I lift them up to You, today.
Lift this burden from me,
give me grace and forgiveness,
That I may know Your love and share it with others,
through your son, Jesus, I pray.
Amen.

Chapter Ten
He's Lord of All

After traveling around the country full time with the group, A Cappella, I came home to Kansas to teach elementary art at several schools, including the one I had attended as a fourth and fifth grader.

All too quickly, I jumped into the routine of working Monday through Friday and living for the weekend where I could sleep late, paint, cook a great breakfast and so on. I found myself living for Fridays and dreading Mondays.

I wasn't even thirty and did not want to spend my time wishing my life away, and wondering what if. What if I were still singing professionally? What if I were able to paint for a living? What if we had started a family and had children? What if God wanted me to be somewhere else doing something different?

I got tired of "iffing." I decided to start living in the moment and praising God whenever I could for everything I could. One moment I praised Him for was at a recent football game.

> *Be deep spirited friends, help others get ahead.*
> *Philippians 2. MSG.*

Love that verse. Love that translation. I've been blessed with deep spirited friends. We discuss our daily schedules, our families, our ups and downs, the Bible, different versions of the Bible (like The Message Bible I used for the scripture above), Christ's sacrifice, and I know that they rejoice when I succeed.

I sat in a college football game with 80,000 others on a beautiful fall day because a deep spirited friend was on the field being honored for his efforts. He has spent years recruiting National Merit Scholars for the college. Which include years of talking to parents and high school students about the benefits of education. Hours on the phone, planning events and schedules, hundreds of lunches with potential students who would end up investing thousands in a university. Today, with the president of the college, he was on the field being honored for his efforts.

I was as proud as a peacock. I wanted to shout to the stadium, or at least let the hundreds of people in our section know, "That's MY friend. I know him." Not only that but we've been at a train station in Kiev, Ukraine, and on the stage in Donetsk singing about the Lord, in a place where it had been proclaimed that there was no God." We've been lost in the woods of Alabama. We've sung the National Anthem on the Fourth of July. We've cried together when we've experienced unbelievable loss.

I wonder if Christ could say that about me? We've been lost together, we've rejoiced together, we've cried together. I know Christ Jesus has been with me through all of life's ups and downs, a deep-spirited friend, who cares about the big things and the little ones. Who trusts me although I've failed Him. Who hopes in me although I've been hopeless. Who believes in me, although I've been faithless.

If you are blessed to have had in your life a deep spirited friend, thank God for them. If you need a deep spirited friend, ask God for one. If you know Jesus, he's waiting to call you his friend.

This was one of the first songs I wrote.

He's Lord of All

I'm tired of livin' for Fridays, tired of dreadin' Mondays
So tired of what this world considers right
I just want to make a difference as I travel here below
I want somehow to let this whole world know

He's Lord of all and Lord of me
And Lord of everything I'm gonna be
Someday I'm gonna see Him in a place I call home
Someday I'll humbly bow before His throne
If I can only show He loves them, I can show they need Him
If I can show how much He's done for me

There'll be no way to stop them from reaching for salvation
They'll be no way to stop loves overflow
Because...

I will be made perfect, all my imperfections gone
The lamb who died will occupy the throne
We'll all glorify Him, free at last from Satan's wrong
We will all join in the victory's song
We'll sing...

Someday I'm gonna meet Him in a place I call home
Someday I'll humbly bow before His throne
Because He's Lord of all

Scriptural Reference:

> *You know the message God sent to the people of Israel, telling the good news of peace through Jesus Christ, who is Lord of all. Acts 10:36. NIV.*

For further reflection:

1. What is one way you can stop dreading Mondays?

2. What is something you are looking forward to?

Prayer for the Day:

God,
Before my life began, You had a plan. Although I can't see around the corner of my future or around the hills that are ahead, I know You are in control. Remind me of that today.
Thank You for knowing I'm human, but loving me anyway.
Through Jesus, your son, I pray.
Amen.

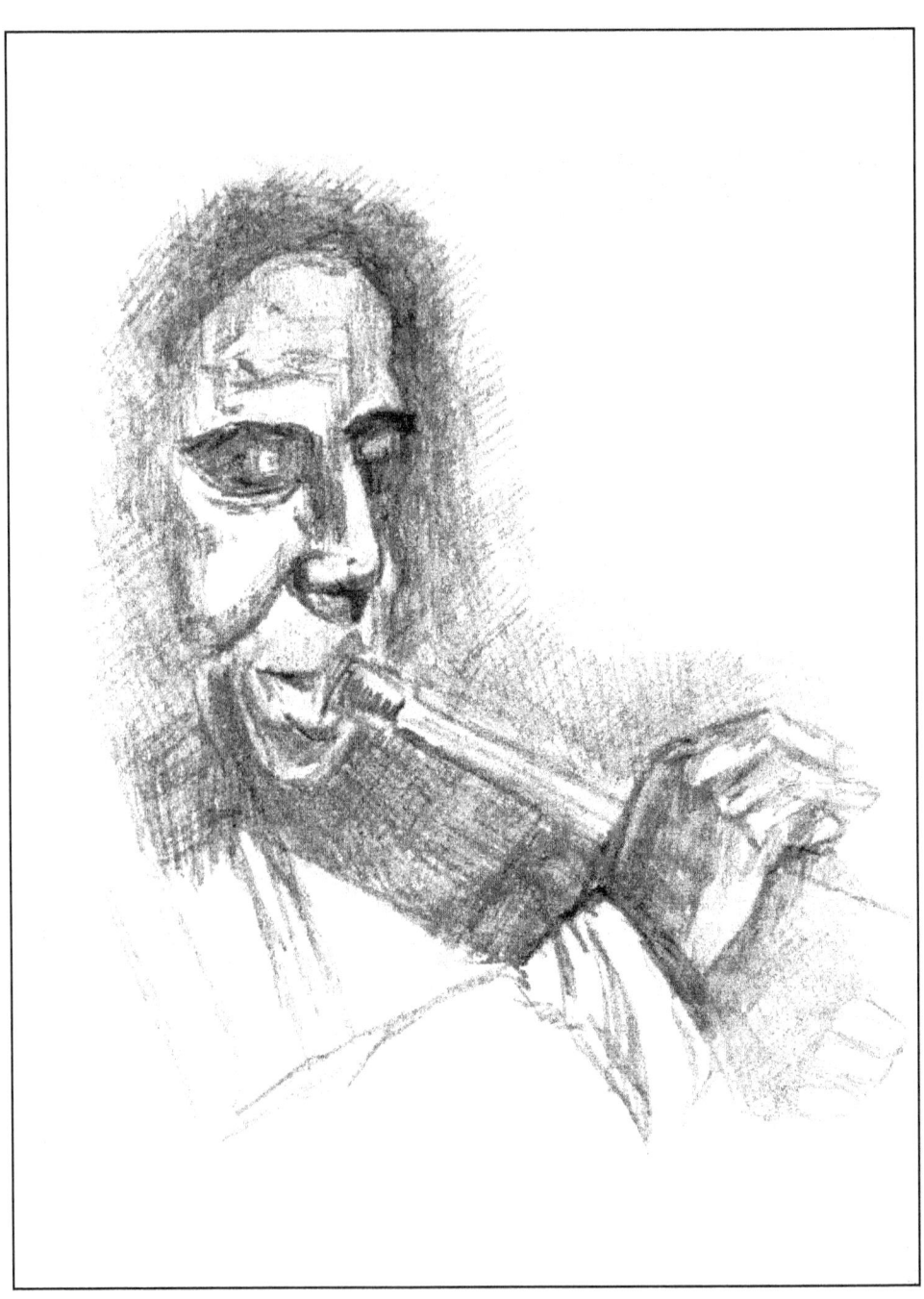

Chapter Eleven
I'm No Picasso

Jackson Pollack, a famous abstract artist was known for his paintings that looked like someone dropped or spilled paint all over a canvas. His paintings sold for five to ten million dollars. A recent discovery of a loft that he painted in, unfolded a toilet seat he had applied his artistic style to. It landed on the internet and fetched over one million dollars. It was not the object that sold for such a high price, it was the artist.

That may seem ridiculous to most of us, but an artist friend of mine, Mark Flickinger, said, "It's not unlike us as Christians. Because the Master has sprinkled, dropped and even covered us with His blood that we become invaluable." That precious blood made us more than a priceless piece of art. It made us holy, blameless and pure. White as snow.

> *For you know that it was not with perishable things such as silver or gold that you were redeemed for the empty way of life handed down to you from your forefathers, but with the precious blood of Christ, a lamb without blemish or defect...*
> *I Peter 1:18-19. NIV.*

I have a unique connection with blood. Since I was diagnosed with diabetes several years ago, I have to check my blood sugar regularly by pricking my finger or my arm to see if my blood sugar is low, normal or high. Different things can affect my blood sugar levels, like stress, illness, food, emotions. It runs the gamut. It can be exhausting and sometimes difficult to tell what it is.

Wouldn't it be interesting if we had a blood tester that determined how the cleansing blood of Jesus Christ was affecting us. If we were low, or not feeling how powerful His sacrifice was, we might be selfish, impatient or even rude.

If our blood level was high, or overflowing with the knowledge of the power of His blood, we might be found doing good. Hopefully, I'd be less legalistic, and self-righteous, and more caring about everyone I come in contact with.

Now I'm no Picasso, or Jackson Pollack but I've created art, analyzed art, and helped thousands of children appreciate art and create art of their own. Children were drawn to Christ. So much so, that when they would crowd around Him, and it concerned His followers, He would have to say,

> *Let the little children come to me, and do not hinder them, for the kingdom of God belongs to such as these.*
> *Luke 18:16. NIV.*

One of my favorite writers used the phrase "no run of the mill Messiah," and it inspired this song:

No Run of the Mill Messiah

He was no run of the mill Messiah, walked the road to Calvary
No average Savior, Jehovah, and Lord is the bread of life for me
No run of the mill Messiah came back to life on the third day
As He promised and said, so He lived and He bled,
Showing He was the truth, life, and way

More than a prophet and more than just a preacher
He was a servant sculpting souls with His hands
More than a carpenter, more than just a teacher
More than an angel and more than a man

Follow His sandal prints and see where they lead us
Smell the sawdust of the carpenter's shop
See the one and only leper thanking Jesus
Of Galilee and born of divine thought

Once you have seen Him, a glimpse of the Savior
You'll long to see Him each day
His words can help us change our behavior
Satan stay out of our way
No run of the mill Messiah

For further reflection:

1. In what way have you shown the love of Jesus to someone recently?

2. In what way could you show Jesus to a family member, or stranger this week?

Prayer for the Day:

Merciful Father,
Just knowing You care enough to send Your son and watch Him suffer so that we can have this relationship with You, humbles me. If I haven't told You today, thank You.
In Your son, Jesus Christ, I pray this prayer,
Amen.

Chapter Twelve
I'm Giving You Pearls

I've never received real pearls, in case you think that is where this chapter is heading. No. One of our favorite sayings is "Listen close, I'm giving you pearls." It's a line from a movie. The character is a retired army colonel and has lost his eyesight. He's at the stage in life where he is trying to pass on his wisdom, and he tells a young man, "I'm givin' you pearls."

I can't help but think of my father and the times he has tried to tell me something important that he learned from life itself, and wanted me to benefit from his experience. You see young people making the same mistakes you have and you want to save them from that experience. As I get older, I realize why people with more maturity want to share their wisdom with you. They want to spare you the pain they've experienced. Don't cast your pearls before swine...

> *Do not give dogs what is sacred, do not throw your pearls to pigs. If you do, they may trample them under feet, and then turn and tear you to pieces.*
> *Matthew 7:6. NIV.*

That scripture comes right before the ask, seek and knock passage. How many times, did Jesus try to explain to His disciples that they were missing the big picture?

Matthew describes a discussion that Jesus had with the disciples after crossing a lake. Beware the yeast of the Pharisees. They discussed among themselves and said, "It's because we didn't bring any bread." That sounds like something I would say at a covered dish dinner. The Son of the Living God is sharing wisdom with His closest followers about the religious people of the day, and all they can come up with is: It's because we forgot to bring bread.

Christ replies, "You of little faith, why are you talking among yourselves about having no bread?" Then several verses later, they understand that He is warning them against the teaching of the Pharisee and Sadducees.

For many reasons, that passage in the gospel gives me hope. Instead of understanding what the Lord of Creation was imparting to them, they began having a chat about bread. Can you see Peter asking the other apostles, "Did you bring the bread? I didn't bring the bread."

"I brought the bread last week," Andrew might have replied. "I knew we couldn't trust John, he never remembers the bread," complains Mark. Sounds like a couple of committees I've been on. The Son of the Living God, hand picked these mere men to share the gospel and they are arguing over carbs.

Must sound like some of the trivial things we fill our minds with as well. Perhaps that's why, of all these things that could have been recorded for us to remember about our Lord and Savior, this passage was included. He didn't pick the perfect. Thank heaven.

For further reflection:

1. Who or where can you turn for encouragement?

2. In what way were the apostles responses similar to ours?

Show Me the Cross

Hundreds of miles, thousands of miracles
The journey to the cross began before Calvary
Angels were silent as the Son of man
Defeated death so we could all be free
Show me the cross
I'll find my way home from there
Show me the cross
It's not to heavy to bear

Show me the cross
All is not lost
I can find my way
Show me the cross
It was no surprise, no hesitation
His death had a purpose, it was meant to be
His parable of grace started in a manger
Led to a cross for eternity
Show me the cross
I'll find my way home from there
Show me the cross
It's not too heavy to bear
Show me the cross
All is not lost
I can find my way
I can find my way
I can find my way
Show me the cross

> *Having canceled the written code, with its regulations, that was against us and that stood opposed to us; he took it away, nailing it to the cross.*
> *Colossians 2:14. NIV.*

Prayer for the Day:

Alpha and Omega,
Beginning and End. Holder of My Hopes. Keeper of My Soul.
Rainbow Maker, Rain Giver, River of Life.
You are so much bigger than I give You credit for.
The little things that I forget to bring to You, that mount up
and become too huge for me to carry anymore,
those things I give to everyone else but you.
Please carry them for me today. My arms are tired.
I know Yours are strong enough ….
Through Jesus I pray,
Amen.

Chapter Thirteen
It Ain't Over...

"I love to hear a big woman sing!" the man in a blue windbreaker proclaimed as he came up to me after we sang at a workshop. Since then I've thought of several replies, "Boy, you sure talk perty." "Bet you say that to all the girls!" or how about, "Does it take a quilt to blow that big nose?"

None of my responses can adequately describe the sharp pain his comment caused to my emotional stability. What possesses people to make that kind of statement to a total stranger? Is there something on my forehead that says, "Humiliate me, please!"

I've had a weight problem since junior high school. I've lost it, gained it, lost it again, but always struggled. I had a great childhood, been blessed with a wonderful family, an amazing husband, and a job I love, and I like to eat. I eat when I'm happy, when I'm sad, when I'm lonely, when I'm with friends. I've never been an alcoholic, but I try to empathize because they can't put the bottle down, and I can't put my fork down.

The man in the blue windbreaker didn't stop with one comment. He continued, "You put those skinny girls to shame. I bet you could sing some opera, couldn't you. Takes a big woman to sing opera."

As he walked away, tears fell down my cheek. My best friend ran over and asked what was wrong. I couldn't even tell her what happened. I was too embarrassed to repeat it. You'd think that would be enough motivation to start fasting right then and there. But it wasn't. I know God made me, and He 'don't make junk.' I know I'm not alone.

> *Some people dig a fork into the pie, but are too lazy to raise it to their mouth.*
> *Proverbs 19:24. MSG.*

Not me. Maybe weight is not your problem. Perhaps you struggle with a shopping addiction, or obsessive compulsive disorder, or you love spreading gossip. Whatever it is that you are struggling with right now, stop for just a moment and make a list of the things you are grateful for. Include the blessings, the simple joys, the air you breathe, a hug from a child, a pat on the back, an e-mail that a friend DIDN'T forward.

I've kept a prayer journal, unfaithfully for several years. I write things down, and then look back months later and realize God already answered that prayer. Then I asked myself, "Did I even thank Him for that one?"

Here's a little poem I wrote for my first great nephew for whom I am so thankful.

Gabe

There's a little boy
Who makes me smile
Just thinking of his face
He brightens every room he's in
Running all around the place
His finger prints are on the door
Just won't wipe them away
Because I know he's growing up
Each and every day
I pray each night that he will be
The man that God has planned
And know that every bump and scrape
Is in the Father's Hands.

For further reflection:

1. What are you grateful for today?

2. Is there a prayer that you are grateful God did not answer yes to?

3. I challenge you to start writing down three things you're grateful for each day. You may find that you will begin looking for more things to be thankful for, and you'll end up wanting to add more to your list than just three.

Prayer for the Day:

Creator, Redeemer and Friend,
Thank You. Today that is enough.
In Jesus name,
Amen.

Chapter Fourteen
Do You Believe?

"If you believe in God, stand up?" my sophomore World History teacher announced. I was in the second row, in a room filled with sleepy high school students, I just assumed people behind me, including my best friend, had stood up with me. Nope. I stood alone.

The teacher continued, "So you believe in God?" "Yes, I do I replied." "You believe that as a Christian, God will forgive all your sins?" "Yes, sir." "So you can just keep on sinning, say you are sorry and you're forgiven?" he prodded. "If my heart is right, yes," I started wondering what the point was. "So you believe if you jump out of this third story window, God will catch you?"

The rest of the class started waking up and wondering how this related to the French Revolution. "If He chooses to," I responded. I started becoming angry that I was the only one on the end of this rampage. Two other students in our class claimed to be Christians, but there was no one else at the brunt of this attack.

"So do it!" he shouted, with his chest sticking out and his hand pointing to the window. "Jump out the window, if you believe God will save you, jump!"

Now, to this day, I'm not sure what prompted my courage, or moved my feet, but I took two steps toward the third story window of our World History Class. The middle-aged atheist educator acted surprised. He shook his head, and with disdain answered, "Sit down, Clover." (That was my maiden name. That's how he addressed each student, unless you were a cheerleader or jock, then you were called by your first name.)

I've never forgotten that day, nor the feeling I had that I was not standing alone. After class, a girl from the tennis team, and the daughter of a local attorney, said, "That took guts, girl. I couldn't have done that."

I share this story in my third book because one of the students, sitting in that class asked me to.

My faith became my own that day. Not my Christian parent's faith, that brought missionaries and Christian College music groups into our home. Not my older sister's faith, that carried her through accident-induced cerebral palsy. Not my Grandpa's faith, that led him through raising ten kids during the Depression.

It became mine. I was willing to stand up, regardless of the costs, or fear, or consequences. I didn't have a gun to my head, like the students at Columbine. But I walked out of that classroom, knowing what kind of teacher I never wanted to be.

In a land of lawsuits and freedom of speech to the point of ridiculousness, that would probably never happen today, but in 1980, things were different.

> ...the eyes of the Lord are in every place, keeping watch on the evil and the good.

For further reflection:

1. Have you ever been persecuted for something you believed in?

> Don't tolerate people who try to run your life, ordering you to bow and scrape, Insisting that you join their obsession with angels and that you seek out visions. They're a lot of hot air, that's all they are. They're completely out of touch with the source of life, Christ, who puts us together in one piece, whose very breath and blood flow through us.
> Colossians 2:18-19. MSG.

2. What have you tolerated in your life that did not emulate following Christ?

3. How can you reach out to someone who is out of touch with the life source?

We had the privilege of singing at a minimum security prison. We sang this song and when we sang the first verse, the inmates responded, "YES!" They took the question literally and responded enthusiastically.

Do You Believe In The Bible

Do you believe in the Bible
Do you believe what it has to say
Oh yes, do you believe in what it teaches
That there is only, there is only one way
If you believe today, then brethren let's all say amen, say amen

Do you believe in Jesus
Do you believe that He died for you and me
Oh yes, do you believe that He died here
On that cruel cross of Calvary
If you believe today then brethren let's all say amen, say amen

Do you believe in one God
Do you believe that He gave His only son
Oh yes, do you believe that Jesus came here
Lord, and died for all that man has done
If you believe today then brethren lets all say amen, say amen

I believe in Jesus, I believe, I believe in Jesus Christ
Oh yes, I believe He gave His precious life
When he made that supreme sacrifice
Yes, If you believe today then won't you with us say amen, say amen.

Prayer for the Day:

God of all good things,
Father of grace and mercy
Help me today to see people the way Christ did.
To love people who are not loveable.
To reach out to those who withdraw from others.
In Your Holy, precious son's name, Jesus,
Amen.

Chapter Fifteen
Slip sliding Away

My husband loves Wyoming. Wide open spaces. Room to roam. Big Sky Country...or is that Montana?

I've always been geographically challenged. I honestly think I was in this time frame when Geography was not taught in school. Perhaps the emphasis was on reading, writing and arithmetic. Two out of three, ain't bad.

Okay, back to Wyoming or Montana. We traveled to sing at a little congregation and we were singing a song my husband Chet wrote, called *Satan's Been Riding Me Hard Blues*, about one of those Sunday Mornings when everything seems to be trying to keep you from making it to church on time. In the middle of the song, my slip fell to the carpet. Evidently the elastic was shot, and I was trying desperately to keep the audience from seeing my embarrassing slip. (A pun intended).

In the process, as I tried to push the slip to the back of the pulpit area, it got hooked on to the black bow on my patent leather shoes, and as I twirled it to try to get it off the shoe, it did not have the desire I planned on. Chet, meanwhile was running the sound system from the back of the church and was unaware of any problem. Everyone else in the group was trying to keep from laughing.

As I recall this story and try to think of what I have learned, I found this scripture:

> *Only hold on to what you have until I come.*
> *Revelation 2:25. NIV.*

"Slip-sliding Away," an old Paul Simon song, was sung most of the way home.

Further reflection:

1. What is something you need to hold on to?

2. What do you need to let go of?

Satan's Been Riding Me Hard Blues

Woke up Sunday morning, I looked at the time, wake up Honey
It's twenty past nine and we're late for church today
I've got those Satan's been riding me so hard blues

Got into the car, everything seemed fine, looked at my speedometer,
I was doing ninety-nine and it's so hard,
See the lights in my rearview mirror
Now Satan's out to get you brother so you better take care
Sitting along side the road policeman says Hi,
look and there's my elders and my deacons
Driving by and it's so hard, don't know what I'm going to do,
I've got the Satan's been riding me so hard blues

Finally got to church headed for my assigned pew,
look and there's a visitor sitting where I'm supposed to,
and it's so hard don't know what I'm going to do
I've got those Satan's been riding me hard blues

Preacher started preaching, his topic that day talking about gossip
Then he looked my way
And it's so hard, about to drive me insane,
Now when it comes to my tongue sister
I've got to keep a tight rein
Invitation was given, thirty stood for the call
Instead of going forward, they just headed for the mall

And it's so hard, don't know what I'm going to do
I've got the Satan's been riding me so hard blues

Now wait a minute, I've got a Savior, He bled and he died
He's always standing right here by my side
And I'm going to praise Him until the day that I die,
And then He's going to take me to that mansion in the sky,
And it's so easy, I know what I'm going to do
I'm going to praise the Lord, How about you?

Prayer for the Day:

Father, I need You now.
I know You hear me.
I know You are seldom early in answering prayers
and You are never late.
I just need to know it's in Your hands,
so I can stop worrying today.
Thank you for knowing what is best for me.
Through Your son Jesus.
Amen.

Chapter Sixteen
Thank God For Kids

Entering my twentieth year of teaching children, I began writing down things that made me chuckle. They say, people who work with kids laugh twenty times more a day, than those who don't. Here's proof.

"My nose is running very fast." Janet, age 7.

Holly, age 6, **"My sister practiced me this."**

While expressing his creative talents, Kaleb, age 6 said, **"I have a background and frontground at the same time."**

"I love art, it's my bestest thing I do!" Riley, age 9.

While making a picture to remember the tragedy of 911, Daulton stated, **"I hope they don't make a holiday out of this."**

"I'm one-fourth American," Spencer, 8.

"My sister's voice is changing, I wonder what her new one will sound like?" Trevor, 6.

After drawing a Santa that didn't turn out like she planned, Latoya said, **"Santa looks like a slow learner."**

"Just because you're not perfect, don't mean your art's not perfect." Amanda, 8.

We spent a class talking about how colors can affect your mood. Red, orange and yellow colors are called warm colors. Blues and greens are considered cool colors.

Joseph, who was nine at the time asked, **"Where did you learn that warm colors radiate? I thought maybe you heard it on the radio."**

Kyle, age seven, describing his classmate, sitting next to him, **"He is blind as a door knob."**

"I swallowed my medicine the first time, that's really good for a kid my age." Kim, age 6.

"These bones ain't what they used to be."
Sharon, 8 years old.

While creating a train picture, Tyler, age 7 said, **"He tooted and three-ted!"**

"I'm an eighth an inch Indian," claimed Raymond, age 9.

We make art for each season and sometimes for certain holidays. As we were making wax resist flag silhouettes, a second grader named Brandon replied, **"They put flags at the cemetery yesterday for Veterinarian's Day."**

Luis, age 9, said, **"American Education Week is when we honor those who died for our country."**

"I've been trying to be the Student of the Week for years and years!"
Kim, age 7

"When I grow up I want to be a *guitogropher.*"
Malcolm, 9

I don't know if that is a guitar player who also takes pictures, or a photographer that only photographs guitars?

"I've been standing here so long I forgot my question,"
Toni 10.

Then there are those pure, honest moments that make you think about what is real:

"Do you know what color Jesus' eyes were?"
nine year old Jason.

Children were drawn to Jesus. They can tell if someone wants them around. They can sense when you are sad or when something is wrong. They sense a closeness and kinship when someone is talking to them on their level or when they see another child their size at a playground or in a classroom.

Whether in a pew at church or standing in line at a store, I've always tried to connect with kids. Maybe with just a smile, or a little drawing of a current cartoon character or just listening. You can learn so much from a child.

For further reflection:

1. How have you become like a child to relate to a child?

2. How have you seen Jesus in a child?

Listen & Obey

Listen and obey that's the Bible way
Listen and obey everyday
Listening to what my parent's say
'Cause that's the Bible way

Everyday I have a list of chores
Picking my clothes and toys off the floor,
Sometimes I fuss and I complain, but that's not the Bible way.
Sometimes it's hard to tell the truth

Doing the things I'm not supposed to do
Hurting my friend by what I say
That's not the Bible way
So I'm going to do my best
Not going to lie or cheat on a test
Helping somebody out each day
'Cause that's the Bible way
Listen and obey that's the Bible way
Listen and obey everyday
Listening to what my parent's say
'Cause that's the Bible way

Prayer for the Day:

Father God,
I come to You as Your child.
Still learning, Still growing,
Still grateful You let me call You father.
In Your son's beautiful name, Jesus Christ, Prince of Peace.
Amen.

Chapter Seventeen
Time for some Pruning

My mother-in-law had beautiful roses. She was so proud of them, and always asked if we noticed them whenever we would visit. I made it a point to start noticing them before we walked though the door.

We now have three beautiful rose bushes outside by our front windows of the house. She would have loved them. She would have known how to help us prune them and would be able to tell if they were getting too much water or not enough.

It's Memorial weekend, and school is almost over. I went out to try to prune our peach tree. Currently my idea of working the land means putting up the plastic swimming pool and reminding my husband to water the marigolds in the flower bed.

I'm not a gardener, nor have I ever run an orchard. I *paint* more trees than I've ever pruned, but it's a cool, cloudy day and I wanted to do something in the yard. I got the clippers out of the shed and went to find dead branches. I just want beautiful peaches that the squirrels or worms don't beat me to.

Being the uneducated pruner I am, I started on the internet. If our dear friend Jack Hamm was still with us, I would ask him about my fruit trees. But he has gone on to Heaven and is watching me from above, trying to guide my hand.

Looking up peach trees, I found out ours has a fungus called Leaf Curl. Took a student of the obvious to see that. Yes, the leaves start curling, and it takes a spray of a fungicide made of lime sulfur and copper sulfate which is to be sprayed in winter, not the last weekend in May.

The Bible talks about branches, vines and pruning.

> *The flowers appear on the Earth, the time of pruning the vines has come, and the song of the dove is heard in our land.*
> *Song of Songs 2:12. NIV.*

John the Apostle, one of the twelve original disciples of Christ, says:

> I am the vine and you are the branches...If anyone does not remain in me, he is like a branch that is thrown away and withers, such branches are picked up, thrown into the fire and burned. If you remain in me and my words remain in you, ask whatever you wish, and it will be given you. This is my Father's glory, that you bear much fruit, showing yourselves to be my disciples."
> John 15:5-8. NIV.

Today, I was clipping the branches that had no leaves or peaches on them. I don't know what they were doing yesterday, or if they had planned on bearing fruit tomorrow. Today was pruning day. I know you are already ahead of me and know where I'm going with this. Whether you shared Jesus with someone five years ago, or even yesterday, what are you doing about sharing him today?

I don't like the idea of pruning. It ranks right up there with criticism, which I've never been good at receiving. However, there's no way to prune gently. If you try to cut off a dead branch slowly, it's like removing a band-aid slowly. It hurts more and pulls at the skin.

One of my favorite songs of all time is the old spiritual entitled *Precious Lord, Take My Hand* by Thomas Andrew Dorsey. Many people thought the song was written by the famous bandleader Tommy Dorsey, but it wasn't. Thomas learned music composition in Chicago, Illinois. He was converted in 1921 and began writing gospel songs but had trouble getting them published. He borrowed five dollars and sent out 500 copies of a song to churches all over the country, and it took three years before he got a single order for the music. He said, "I felt like going back to the blues." (Morgan, 2003) But he didn't, and his work became well known.

While leading music in St. Louis, Missouri, he was given a telegram saying his wife had just died. A friend drove him through the night to his home, only to learn that his baby boy had also died. He said he felt God had done him a great injustice, and he didn't want to serve Him anymore. By the next Sunday, a stillness came over him and the words began to fall into place like drops of water falling from the crevice of a rock. He is remembered as the Father of Gospel Music and went on to write hundreds of songs including *Peace in the Valley*.

When we recorded *Precious Lord, Take My Hand* my husband sang lead. He has an amazing voice, and it still gives me goose bumps when I hear him sing it. We sang it at his Grandpa Doolittle's funeral, and I will never forget it.

Precious Lord, Take My Hand

Precious Lord, take my hand
Lead me on, let me stand
I am tired, I am weak, I am worn
Through the storm, through the night
Lead me on to the light
Take my hand precious Lord, lead me home

When my way grows drear, precious Lord linger near
When my life is almost gone
Hear my cry, hear my call
Hold my hand lest I fall
Take my hand precious, Lord, lead me home

When the shadows appear and the night draws near
And the day is past and gone
At the river I'll stand
Guide my feet, hold my hand
Take my hand, precious Lord lead me home.

For further reflection:

1. Can you recall a time when you were criticized unjustly?

2. Can you remember a time when you were pruned and it was needed?

Prayer for the Day:

Our Heavenly Father, also knows about pruning.
He knows when to cut,
how deeply, and how to nourish in between times.
He knows when we need a shoulder to cry on,
or a song of encouragement,
or a friend's phone call at just the right time.
In Jesus name, I lift this prayer to You,
Amen.

Chapter Eighteen
Sing It Out

This scripture was quoted in church last week, and I underlined it:

> *So thank God for His marvelous love, for His miracle mercy to the children He loves. Offer thanksgiving sacrifices, tell the world what He's done--- sing it out!*
> *Psalm 107: 22. MSG.*

I haven't sung it out this week. I haven't even whispered it. It was one of those weeks, when every sound, seemed to get on my nerves. We were eating at our favorite restaurant, and the phones were ringing, and the owners were moving into the apartment upstairs, right above our heads. I asked my husband, "Is it just me?" Even the waitress commented on how noisy it was. I just wanted it to stop.

I wondered what I had been put on the planet to do. Students were not listening. Of course, the last week of school, they rarely do. Even the teachers were loud. They were more ready to be out of school than anyone.

I was just exhausted.

Then a call came in yesterday morning. A congregation wanted us to come and sing, near Wichita, Kansas, and I called to confirm that a date would work for us, and our contact person called back to tell me she had received my message. Then she asked us to pray.

It seems a young couple was driving home from Colorado for the holiday weekend, and a tornado came through. The couple had pulled over because of the rain. They were picked up by the tornado and thrown 150 yards away from the highway. The car wasn't found until this morning, as it was in a wheat field. Both of them were killed, and the husband's father is the minister of the congregation we were just asked to sing for.

    I thought about the parents who had been waiting for their son and daughter-in-law to get home. I wondered how long they had to wait until they heard the news.

    I thought about how unpredictable the weather in Kansas is, and how we've become desensitized to Tornado Warnings. It just seems like there is a warning every evening from April to August, and you glance up at the television and notice it is no where near your county, so you go on.

    Then the realization hit me. That red car that was mangled that just came across the news, was theirs. Two lives that I did not know, had just touched mine.

> So I stopped.
> I prayed.
>   I prayed for the family, the minister, and his wife
>   who've lost their son.
>   Help my mother's throat to heal.
>   Bring down my dad's blood pressure.
>   Watch over my nephew.
>   Help my husband with his new job.

Before that phone call I hadn't just stopped during the day, or even before I went to sleep to say "Thank you, Lord."

We're under another Tornado Warning. The clouds are dark and rolling in from the north. The temperature has dropped twelve degrees in the last hour and Lord, I want to thank You....

> Thank You for the ceiling fan over my bed.
> Thank You for sandals that fit and feel comfy on my feet after a long day.
> Thank You for warm water in the shower and Sonic ice in a diet cherry limeade.
> Thank You for my family that cares when I've had a bad day.
> Thank You for protecting our home during the 45 mile per hour winds.
> Thank You for Your son, Jesus and the sacrifice He made.

Thank You for calling me Your child.

...tell the world what He's done, sing it out!

You've Got to Go

> *Jesus did not let him, but said, "Go home to your family and tell them how much the Lord has done for you and how he has had mercy on you. So the man went away and began to tell in the Decapolis how much Jesus had done for him. And all the people were amazed.*
> *Mark 5:19-20. NIV.*

In Mathew, Mark and Luke we find the story of the time when on the water near the land of Gerasenes, the disciples were with Jesus when they heard some awful moaning and the holler came from back behind the trees.
The man had lived among the tombs but chains could not subdue him both night and day he cut himself and cried. Right away the demons knew the majesty among them for the Son of God was who they recognized

You've got to go, go tell what the Lord has done for you
You've got to go, go tell what the Lord has done for you
His mercy never ends and He will always see you through
You've got to go, go tell what the Lord has done for you

The demons that were in him had become so panic stricken driving him out of his right and normal mind. But their previous location must have been so very awful that they begged the Lord to put them in the swine.
The plan was not effective and the pigs began a running and their destination was catastrophe once the stampede had got started there was just no way to stop it and the pigs began to fly into the sea.
The people of the region came to see the brand new Legion, out of chains and acting like an average Joe, sitting there beside the preacher and with one outstanding feature he was actually even wearing clothes but the people became frightened and began to plead with Jesus we were better off before you even came, but Legion begged to differ and he wanted to go with him, the one who changed him from lunatic to sane.

You've got to go, go tell what the Lord has done for you
You've got to go, go tell what the Lord has done for you
His mercy never ends and He will always see you through
You've got to go, go tell what the Lord has done for you

For further reflection:

1. What is your favorite hymn or song, and why does it touch you?

2. When in your life have you experienced a tragedy that brought you to your knees?

Prayer for the Day:

Elohim-the All Powerful One,
Designer of the Universe,
thank You for the beauty You let me experience.
Thank You for the tragedy that You have protected me from
and led me through.
In the name of Your son who sacrificed His life for mine, Lord Jesus.
Amen.

Chapter Nineteen
Cat Herding

If you've ever tried to rush a two year old, you are barking up the wrong tree. The faster you wish to move, the faster they go in the wrong direction. They go where and when they want to go. I now understand those little maps that Bill Hearne draws in the newspaper cartoon *Family Circle*. It's a lot like herding cats. You just don't. They don't follow like sheep and can not be led.

When our cat is outside after dark, I'm concerned that a coyote or neighbor dog might consider her a midnight snack. We plan this whole escapade, where my husband will go out the front door and go around the porch trying to encourage her to come in on her own, like a border collie gentle nudging the sheep into the fenced in farm yard. Eventually, she makes her way in, but occasionally I take a package of Whiskas cat food and rattle the wrapper so she'll come running.

> *Gently encourage the stragglers and reach out for the exhausted, pulling them to their feet.*
> *I Thessalonians 5:14. MSG.*

Ironically I found my great nephew acts in a similar way when I hold out a package of goldfish crackers. He temporarily forgets what was so important just minutes before, and comes running. Sometimes life takes motivation. We need encouragement to do what should be done.

My cousin, Lezlie had a framed saying in her home that read something like this:

The best education of any, is doing what you have to do, even when you don't want to do it.

I've reflected on that many times. When I've been asked to sing at a funeral and my heart is hurting so badly I just want to cover my head and go back to bed. When I know I should apologize for something I've said, but my pride keeps the words from coming out of my mouth.

The Apostle Paul says to encourage and reassure one another with these words:

> *Speak encouraging words to one another. Build up hope so you'll all be together in this -no one left out, no one left behind.*
> *I Thessalonians 5:10. MSG.*

I see children who think it's fun to be in a club, or select group, and have a secret password. I hear almost daily, the childhood taunt, "If you don't.....then I won't be your friend." Too often, we act the same way as adults, we just don't say it so simply.

We had an ark. It's true, like Noah, we had our very own ark. My dad took an old plywood boat and built a play house on top of it. Then he took a Rambler dashboard and put it in the front of the ark so we could pretend to steer.

My sister and I would play for hours in our ark.

This may explain why I still enjoy driving today.

A little neighbor girl would come over to play, but we were a few years older and would tell her she didn't know the password. Although she is now a physician's assistant, I'm still reminded of how we made her feel left out and excluded. (So sorry, Jami.)

> *God didn't set us up for an angry rejection, but for salvation by our Master, Jesus Christ.*
> *I Thessalonians 5:9. NIV.*

The church is not about keeping people out, but bringing people in. I've been in too many churches where they did not make you feel welcome. In fact they advertised how many people they had 'withdrawn' from in the same way they posted the songs for the Sunday worship service.

I find it interesting that the gospel is vague enough to be applicable two thousand years ago, but also specific enough to help us follow the path of light today.

I was in an audience of over a thousand Christians in Tulsa, Oklahoma. The song leader said, "God is Good?" and without hesitation the audience replied, "All the Time." The leader continued, "All the time," and the crowd responded, "God is Good." I had goosebumps and this song was on my heart soon after.

God Is Good, All The Time

God is good, all the time
You know and all the time my God is good
When life don't work out like it should
I still know my God is good

Noah heard it was going to rain
The neighbors thought he'd gone insane
When the lightning came and the thunder shook
Noah said, yeah, my God is good

Jonah thought he had himself a plan
But he didn't listen to the Lord's command
Within three days his goals had changed
The Lord sure works in mysterious ways

Rahab thought that her time had come
Until the spies came to her home
Then a red cord showed the way
To save her family on that day

For further reflection:

1. When have you felt angry or rejected?

2. How does Christ's sacrifice soothe that pain?

3. How has Jesus felt the way you've felt before?

Prayer for the Day:

Mighty One,
Thank You for loving me in spite of myself.
Through the perfect blood of Jesus,
Amen.

Chapter Twenty
Things to do

My To Do List grows weekly. Priorities change, time races on, but here is a list I've had for awhile.

My To Do List

See the redwoods in California and marvel at their size and
    beauty.
Watch my great nephews play soccer or sing in a choir.
Tell my husband how grateful I am he not only puts up with me,
    but is also a tremendous encourager.
Paint a realistic landscape with clouds that look real.
Thank my parents for showing me Jesus.
See the Grand Canyon.
Take a Braum's hamburger with raw onions to my grandma.
Update our website with a blog, when I figure out how to blog.
Toss the old make up in the top drawer of my dresser.
Find someone who can use size eleven shoes.
Paint a Kansas sunset.
Write a handwritten letter to my friend.
Get rid of the socks that don't have a match, or turn them into
    sock puppets.
See the Mona Lisa.
Cook a whole meal as well as my friend, Jaynell.
Sit on the back porch at Mom and Dad's and rock in the rocking
    chairs without watching the clock.

You probably have your own to do list. I've included mine for a couple of reasons:
  A. So I can remember what I need to do.
  B. So you will realize how mundane life can be.
  C. So you will realize how priceless life can be.
  D. Lastly, if I don't get around to everything on my list, people I love will know ...
  I meant well.

For further reflection:

1. What is number one on your life to do list?

2. What is one thing you are glad you have already done?

3. What's on your to-do list that you really feel you must accomplish in your lifetime?

4. What are you doing today that really won't matter in five years?

A preacher was giving a lesson from Isaiah 53. The words sounded like poetry to me. Some songs write themselves. This is one that did.

It Was His Will

It was His will His Son would suffer
It was His will He'd take the blame
There simply could not be another
The Lamb of God for us was slain
He had no special beauty, no attraction for to see
Nothing in His appearance, no sign of majesty
Despised, also rejected, by men He came to save
Pierced for our transgression while showing us the way

Like sheep who've left the shepherd, each to his separate way
The lamb was led to slaughter, the priceless gift was paid
No word was said in anger, no violence had He done
He bore the sins of many, the Father's only Son
Carrying our burdens all alone
The Father turned His head so sin could be atoned
No one to the rescue, 'cause He was on His own
The plan of man's salvation to unfold

There simply could not be another
The Lamb of God for us was slain

> *And He made known to us the mystery of His will according to His good pleasure, which He purposed in Christ, to be put into effect when the times will have reached their fulfillment--to bring all things in heaven and on Earth together under one head, even Christ.*
> *Ephesians 1:9-10. NIV.*

Prayer for the Day:

Granter of grace and mercy,
You are almighty and amazing. You are my Lord and my God.
I give You the praise and the honor for all that You've done.
Thank You in advance for all You will do.
You alone, know what I need, and when I need it.
Thank you.
In Your son's name I pray,
Amen.

Chapter Twenty-One
God's Grace and Gummy worms

(Read only if you are a mother, daycare provider, Sunday School or pre-school teacher, or have ever been a babysitter.)

For all you do, this chapter is for you. Thank you.

I just spent one week watching an 18 month old and a 3 ½ year old. I love them more than life, but I am exhausted.

Today, I've changed two dirty diapers.
Filled five sippy cups,
Watched *Thomas and the Magic Railroad* three times.
Watched the dancing penguin section of the animated movie,
    Happy Feet, two times.
Been surprised by my sister and mother hiding in the Burger
    King playground.
Like I needed one more surprise.
Put socks on little feet, four times.
Moved a child's car seat twice, which should be a requirement
    for any engineer to graduate.
I've been through one entire package of baby wipes.
I've done three loads of laundry.
I've tried to make pull-ups fit like diapers, and they don't.
Scotch tape does not work as well as packing tape.
I've not finished one bottle of water without half of it filling up
    my car seat or the ottoman.

I've learned that sugar-free Jell-O stains worse than any-flavor Kool-Aid.
Unwrapped Tootsie Pops really do stick to anything.
Cat food looks like trail mix if you're under two.
Lastly, there is a Lightning McQueen race car in our bass speaker of the surround sound system, that my husband probably won't find until he reads this.

I take my hat off to anyone who cares for children on a regular basis. I don't know how you do it. I've laughed, cried, begged, endured gum in my hair, pop tarts in the loveseat, Cheetos in my bed, and questions no human can answer.

A sign above a crib in a church nursery quoted this scripture:

> ....We shall not all sleep, but we shall all be changed...
> I Corinthians 15:51. NIV.

You can't go to the bathroom, to the kitchen, to the laundry room, to the store, to the mailbox, without a trail of blankets, shirt tugs, and spills. How any of us actually make it to puberty, is only through God's grace and gummy worms.

Faithful to the End

Faithful, faithful to the end
Holding on to the Savior's hand
Comes a time you must take a stand
So be faithful, faithful to the end

By faith a baby takes a step
Though falling causes pain
Practice making permanent
This painful walking game

I stumble like a child at times
And getting up's so very tough
But falling brings me to my knees
And I'm not there near enough

The trials come upon us
We stand the test of time
We run or will we falter
Our faith's the bottom line
Christ will dwell in your heart
If you have the faith
If you have the faith

For further reflection:

1. How forgiving are you of yourself when you slip and fall?

2. How forgiving are you of others?

Prayer for the Day:

Father of all things, creator of our hopes and dreams:
Thank You for blessing our lives with those who cared for us
when we were young.
Thank You for those who prayed over us as children.
Thank You for the children in my life.
From Your child, through Your son, Jesus,
Amen.

Afterword

We found out as I was finishing this book, that my mother was diagnosed with ALS, also known as Lou Gehrig's Disease.

If you get my sense of humor, it's from my mama.
If you've seen my hair color, it's from my mama.
If you've heard me laugh, it's from my mama.
If you've seen my drawings, it's because of my mama.
For any good I have done, it's because of my parent's love and example.
Never have two people done so much to help so many. Our home was filled with missionaries, singing groups, preachers, Bible studies, card games, and fellowship.
I'm so blessed to have seen her teach, speak, organize, give and love unconditionally.

We would be grateful for your prayers as God leads us through this next chapter of our lives.

GOD IS GOOD, ALL THE TIME.

Prayer:

Father God ,
My head is bowed, my shoulders are relaxed,
and my heart is exhausted.
Waiting for a few hours at the doctors today
to hear if a loved one has a life altering diagnosis.
I know You are in all and above all.
I'm grateful You hold the hands of Your children through such times.
I know we are not alone.
Thank You.
Amen.

Bibliography

All verses quoted come from one or the other of these two versions of the Holy Bible:

International Bible Society. *New International Version, Holy Bible.* Zondervan Publishers, 1984.

Peterson, Eugene. *The Message: The Bible in Contemporary Language.* NavPress Publishing Group, 2002.

Chapter One:

Or suppose a woman has ten silver coins and loses one. Does she not light a lamp, sweep the house and search carefully until she find it?
Luke 15:8-10. NIV.

But store up for yourselves treasures in heaven, where moth and rust do not destroy, and where thieves do not break in and steal. For where your treasure is, there your heart will be also.
Matthew 6:21. New International Version (NIV).

Chapter Two:

I tell you the truth, unless you change and become like little children, you will never enter the kingdom of Heaven.
Matthew 18:2. NIV.

Since, then, you have been raised with Christ, set your hearts on things above, where Christ is seated at the right hand of God.
Colossians 3:1. NIV.

Chapter Three:

Thy word is a lamp unto my feet and a light unto my path...
Psalm 119:105. NIV.

Therefore, my dear friends, as you have always obeyed-not only in my presence, but now much more in my absence-continue to work out your salvation with fear and trembling, for it is God who works in you to will and to act according to his good purpose.
Philippians 2:12-13. NIV.

Chapter Four:

It's not the one who plants or the one who waters who is at the center of this process, but God, who makes things grow.
I Corinthians 3:8. The Message Bible (MSG).

Chapter Five:

God wants you to mature, God doesn't want his children holding grudges.
Philippians 4:2. MSG .

With each of you we were like a father with his child, holding your hand, whispering encouragement, showing you step by step, how to live well before God who called you into His own kingdom and into this delightful life.
I Thessalonians 2:11. MSG.

So come on, let's leave finger-painting exercises on Christ and get on with the grand work of art.
Hebrews 6:1. MSG.

Let the peace of Christ rule in your hearts, since as members of one body you were called to peace. And be thankful.
Colossians 3:15. NIV.

Whatever you do, work at it with all of your heart, as working for the Lord, not for men.
Colossians 3:23. NIV.

Chapter Six:

Since we live by the Spirit, let us keep in step with the Spirit.
Galatians 5:25. NIV.

Chapter Seven:

I do not understand what I do. For what I want to do I do not do, but what I hate I do. And if I do what I do not want to do, I agree that the law is good. And it is, it is no longer I myself who do it, but it is sin living in me. I know that nothing good lives in me, that is in my sinful nature. For I have the desire to do what is good, but I cannot carry it out. For what I do is not the good I want to do, nor the evil I do not want to do--this I keep on doing.
Romans 7:15-19. NIV.

He says, 'I will declare your name to my brothers; in the presence of the congregation I will sing your praises.'
Hebrews 2:12. NIV.

Finally brothers live in harmony one with another .
I Peter 3:8. NIV.

Chapter Eight:

So he got up and went to his father. But while he was still a long way off, his father saw him and was filled with compassion for him; he ran to his son, threw his arms around him and kissed him.
Luke 15:20. NIV.

Chapter Nine:

When the light of the lamp shines on you. See to it then that the light within you is not darkness. Don't hide your light.
Luke 11:35. NIV.

A city on a hill cannot be hidden. Neither do people light a lamp and put it under a bowl. Instead they put it on its stand, and it gives light to everyone in the house.
Matthew 5:14-15. NIV.

Where, O death, is your victory? Where, O death, is your sting?
I Corinthians 15:55. NIV.

Chapter Ten:

You know the message God sent to the people of Israel, telling the good

news of peace through Jesus Christ, who is Lord of all.
Acts 10:36. NIV.

Chapter Eleven:

For you know that it was not with perishable things such as silver or gold that you were redeemed for the empty way of life handed down to you from your forefathers, but with the precious blood of Christ, a lamb without blemish or defect..
I Peter 1:18-19. NIV.

Let the little children come to me, and do not hinder them, for the kingdom of God belongs to such as these.
Luke 18:16. NIV.

Chapter Twelve:

Do not give dogs what is sacred, do not throw your pearls to pigs. If you do, they may trample them under feet, and then turn and tear you to pieces.
Matthew 7:6. NIV.

Ask and it will be given to you; Seek and you will find; Knock and the door will be opened to you.
Matthew 7:7. NIV.

Having canceled the written code, with its regulations, that was against us and that stood opposed to us; he took it away, nailing it to the cross.
Colossians 2:14. NIV.

Chapter Thirteen :

Some people dig a fork into the pie, but are too lazy to raise it to their mouth.
Proverbs 19:24. MSG.

Chapter Fourteen:

...the eyes of the Lord are in every place, keeping watch on the evil and the good.
Proverbs 15:3. MSG.

Don't tolerate people who try to run your life, ordering you to bow and scrape, insisting that you join their obsession with angels and that you seek out visions. They're a lot of hot air, that's all they are. They're completely out of touch with the source of life, Christ, who puts us together in one piece, whose very breath and blood flow through us.
Colossians 2:18-19. MSG.

Chapter Fifteen:

Simon, Paul. "Slip Slidin' Away," *Paul Simon's Greatest Hits.* Warner Brothers, 1977.

Only hold on to what you have until I come.
Revelation 2:25. NIV.

Chapter Seventeen:

Morgan, Robert J. "Precious Lord, Take My Hand," *Then Sings My Soul,* p. 289. Thomas Nelson Publishers, 2003.

The flowers appear on the Earth, the time of pruning the vines has come, and the song of the dove is heard in our land.
Song of Songs 2:12. NIV.

I am the vine and you are the branches...If anyone does not remain in me, he is like a branch that is thrown away and withers, such branches are picked up, thrown into the fire and burned. If you remain in me and my words remain in you, ask whatever you wish, and it will be given you. This is my Father's glory, that you bear much fruit, showing yourselves to be my disciples.
John 15:5-8. NIV.

Chapter Eighteen:

So thank God for His marvelous love, for His miracle mercy to the children He loves, offer thanksgiving sacrifices, tell the world what He's done--- sing it out!
Psalm 107:22. MSG.

Jesus did not let him, but said, "Go home to your family and tell them how much the Lord has done for you and how he has had mercy on

you. So the man went away and began to tell in the Decapolis how much Jesus had done for him. And all the people were amazed.
Mark 5:19-20. NIV.

Chapter Nineteen:

Gently encourage the stragglers and reach out for the exhausted, pulling them to their feet.
I Thessalonians 5:14. MSG.

Speak encouraging words to one another. Build up hope so you'll all be together in this -no one left out, no one left behind.
I Thessalonians 5:10. MSG.

God didn't set us up for an angry rejection, but for salvation by our Master, Jesus Christ.
I Thessalonians 5:9. MSG.

Chapter Twenty:

And he made known to us the mystery of His will according to His good pleasure, which He purposed in Christ, to be put into effect when the times will have reached their fulfillment--to bring all things in heaven and on Earth together under one head, even Christ.
Ephesians 1:9-10. NIV.

Chapter Twenty-One

....We shall not all sleep, but we shall all be changed...
I Corinthians 15:51. NIV.

Other Books By Danice E. Sweet

Floating Zoo and the Whale Motel. Corpus Christi: Pearson Publishing Company, 2006.

Consider It Joy. Corpus Christi: Pearson Publishing Company, 2007.

Danice E. Sweet

Danice is an author, illustrator, painter, song writer and singer. She has been a public school art instructor for the past twenty years. She is also the author and illustrator of *Consider It Joy* and the children's book *Floating Zoo and the Whale Motel* published by Pearson Publishing Company in 2007 and 2006 respectively. As in the other two books, Danice is giving to purchasers a CD recording of her original songs mentioned in the book (coupon inside the book). She sings professionally with her group, Revival, who tour the United States and Canada, and have performed in the Ukraine.

PEARSON PUBLISHING COMPANY
CORPUS CHRISTI, TEXAS

For a complete list and description of our publications and to order books, please go to our website:

www.PearsonPub.US

Saga of a Comanche Warrior: Book One
Little Boy
By Max Oliver $12.95

Slumbertime: A Parent's Guide for Children's Sleep and Sleep Problems
By Janet S. Gould $29.95

Catching the Dream: A Parent's Guide for Children's Dreams
By Janet S. Gould $26.95

Deal Me In
By Alyce Guynn with illustrations by Jesse Taylor $23.95

His Angels Are In Charge
By Frances Cotten Woodard $24.95

Floating Zoo and the Whale Motel
Written & Illustrated By Danice Sweet $26.95

Consider It Joy
Written & Illustrated By Danice Sweet $16.95

I Will Speak Your Name
Written & Illustrated By Danice Sweet $16.95

To mail in orders, send (1) a list of titles with number of copies of each title, (2) check or money order for total retail price of all books, plus (3) $5.00 shipping and handling for each book, and (4) your name and mailing address printed clearly, to:

Pearson Publishing Company
555 S. Shoreline Blvd., Suite 104
Corpus Christi, Texas 78401

Music CD included with book purchase.

To receive your recording of author Danice Sweet and her group, Revival, singing her songs which she discusses in this book, fill out this coupon and mail it to the address below.

PLEASE PRINT

Name: _____

Street Address: _____

City, State, Zip Code: _____

MAIL TO:

Pearson Publishing Company
555 S. Shoreline Blvd., Suite 104
Corpus Christi, Texas 78401

www.ingramcontent.com/pod-product-compliance
Lightning Source LLC
Chambersburg PA
CBHW072159100426
42738CB00011BA/2469